Oliver Cromwell: The Notorious Life and Legacy of the Lord Protector of the Commonwealth of England

By Charles River Editors

A 1656 portrait of Cromwell

About Charles River Editors

Charles River Editors provides superior editing and original writing services across the digital publishing industry, with the expertise to create digital content for publishers across a vast range of subject matter. In addition to providing original digital content for third party publishers, we also republish civilization's greatest literary works, bringing them to new generations of readers via ebooks.

Sign up here to receive updates about free books as we publish them, and visit Our Kindle Author Page to browse today's free promotions and our most recently published Kindle titles.

Introduction

A 1649 portrait of Cromwell

Oliver Cromwell (1599-1658)

"Necessity hath no law. Feigned necessities, imagined necessities...are the greatest cozenage that men can put upon the Providence of God, and make pretenses to break known rules by." – Oliver Cromwell

"Put your trust in God, my boys, but keep your powder dry." – attributed to Oliver Cromwell

For over a thousand years, England has had a monarchy, and though the line of succession did not always pass smoothly, it has almost always been continuous. England has more often been faced with the claims of competing kings and queens than with a period of no monarch at all. The major exception to that rule came in the 11 years between 1649 and 1660, when England was a republic. Following the disastrous reign of Charles I and the civil wars that led to his execution, Parliament and the army ruled England. England's republican experiment started out as a work of collaboration and compromise; lords, army officers and members of Parliament (MPs) worked together to find a political settlement that did not include the despised royal House of Stuart.

Nonetheless, religious and political division made collective rule unworkable, and ultimately, one man emerged from the chaos to rule the country. He had risen from a humble background to become the leading general of the Civil Wars, and as a man of staunch beliefs and ruthless pragmatism, he controlled England from 1653-1658 under the title of Lord Protector. In essence, he was a king in all but name.

That man was Oliver Cromwell, and in the popular imagination, Cromwell has overshadowed the rest of the leaders of the parliamentary cause and the New Model Army. His name is known by everyone in England, while parliamentary leaders like John Pym, constitutional reformers like John Lambert, and even Sir Thomas Fairfax, who led Parliament's army through most of the wars, are known only to history buffs. But Cromwell has also been one of the most controversial figures in English history ever since. Viewed by some as a despot and others as a champion of liberty, Cromwell's legacy is so diverse that while many Irish accuse him of genocide, others look at him as a social revolutionary.

Even in England, Cromwell was both a beloved and reviled figure, with seemingly no middle ground. One 17th century English writer thunderously denounced him as the "English monster, the center of mischief, a shame to the British Chronicle, a pattern for tyranny, murder and hypocrisie, whose bloody Tyranny will quite drown the name of Nero, Caligula, Domitian, having at last attained the height of his Ambition, for Five years space he wallowed in the blood of many Gallant and Heroick Persons." As if to put the exclamation point on his divisive legacy, Cromwell went from being buried as a national hero in Westminster Abbey in 1658 to being exhumed and having his corpse symbolically executed and beheaded in public by supporters of the Royalists in 1660. Even the location of Cromwell's decapitated head continues to be a source of debate and interest among Britons.

To this day Cromwell is a hugely divisive figure, hated by the Irish for his brutality, loathed by monarchists, but admired by republicans and English reformers. A film was released in 1970 celebrating his political career, and St Ives, one of his home towns, is host to a statue of the man. Of course, some observers recognize contradictions in Cromwell, such as the 20th century Scottish writer John Buchan, who may have summed the Lord Protector's life up best: "A devotee of law, he was forced to be often lawless; a civilian to the core, he had to maintain himself by the sword; with a passion to construct, his task was chiefly to destroy; the most scrupulous of men, he had to ride roughshod over his own scruples and those of others; the tenderest, he had continually to harden his heart; the most English of our greater figures, he spent his life in opposition to the majority of Englishmen; a realist, he was condemned to build that which could not last."

Oliver Cromwell: The Notorious Life and Legacy of the Lord Protector of the Commonwealth of England chronicles the tumultuous life of one of England's most important figures. Along with pictures and a bibliography, you will learn about Cromwell like never before, in no time at all.

Oliver Cromwell: The Notorious Life and Legacy of the Lord Protector of the Commonwealth of England

About Charles River Editors

Introduction

   Chapter 1: Early Years

   Chapter 2: The Road to War

   Chapter 3: The First Civil War

   Chapter 4: A Failed Peace

   Chapter 5: The Second Civil War

   Chapter 6: The Commonwealth

   Chapter 7: Lord Protector

   Chapter 8: Death and Succession

   Chapter 9: Cromwell's Legacy

Bibliography

Chapter 1: Early Years

"I was by birth a gentleman, living neither in considerable height, nor yet in obscurity." – Oliver Cromwell

Born on April 25, 1599 in Huntingdon, Oliver Cromwell was the son of Robert Cromwell and Elizabeth Steward, and despite being the fifth of 10 children, he was the only boy in the family to survive infancy in an era when child mortality was still quite high. The Cromwell's were descended from a sister of Thomas Cromwell (c.1485-1540), a famous minister for King Henry VIII. The family had become wealthy during the Reformation when they took over property confiscated by Henry VIII from the church, and though they switched between the surnames of Williams and Cromwell, by the 1590s they were well settled within the landed gentry of Huntingdonshire in the English East Midlands.

Portrait of Thomas Cromwell

Oliver's grandfather, Sir Henry Williams, was the second richest landowner in the county, but while he had many children, Robert was one of the younger ones, so he inherited only a small portion of land and a house in Huntingdon. This left the Cromwell's still part of the landed gentry but in its lower tier, with an income from the land of up to £300 per year.

England at the time was a very hierarchical country. Someone of Oliver's birth could be expected to live comfortably but never to make a huge name for himself. As Cromwell himself later put it, he was destined to live 'neither in considerable height, nor yet in obscurity'. This was a time in England's history when political, social and economic leadership were almost entirely dictated by birth. An aristocrat might rise from the lower ranks of the nobility to the upper ones, or go down the other way. A small merchant might become moderately wealthy, but most people never left the station in which they were born, and for the vast majority this meant a life as a peasant farmer, working the land, attending church on Sunday, and seldom traveling more than a dozen miles from home.

However, while the lives of ordinary people remained stable and unchanging, people of power and influence were trying to maintain power in tumultuous times. The growth in artistic and intellectual endeavour unleashed by the Renaissance meant that ideas were growing and changing faster than at any point in history. The 16th century had then seen the rise of the Protestant Reformation across the continent, and in some regions, including England, Protestants had gone from oppressed heretics to the dominant religious group, while the Catholic Church and its supporters eagerly fought back. A growth in international exploration and trade was also causing economic upheaval. Inevitably these changes created conflicts, conflicts which sometimes spiraled into violence and even war, and though no one could have predicted it at his birth, these changes would come to define Oliver Cromwell's life and legacy.

Like the vast majority of people in England at the time, the Cromwell's were Christian, and Oliver was christened four days after his birth. Even in England, separated by sea from its neighbors, religious reform and controversy were in the air. The Protestant reform movement was shaking Europe, with theologians following the teachings of Calvin and Luther and preaching a radical reformation of the church, away from the old Catholic hierarchies and towards a new approach in which each Christian had access to God's word through translations of the Bible. In England, this was accompanied by King Henry VIII's break from the authority of the Pope, setting up a separate Church of England, but this was a church founded on political rather than doctrinal ideology, and while some preachers were trying to push it towards the Protestant extreme of Puritanism, others favored a far more elaborate Catholic-style religion referred to as Arminianism. England's religious divisions were awkward ones, and for that reason the monarch and their advisers often avoided tackling them. At the same time, however, this meant the divisions were allowed to grow.

From around 1604, Oliver attended Huntingdon Grammar School, where he was taught by Puritan scholar Thomas Beard. Beard became a friend of the family and a big influence on Oliver, and his presence in the young man's life is indicative both of the family's religious leanings and of the direction Oliver's faith would eventually take him in. He was growing up in a tradition which challenged authority, even while enforcing a strict moral code that was quick to preach the word of righteousness and condemn its opponents.

After Huntingdon, Cromwell went up to Cambridge, where he studied at Sidney Sussex College. The college had been founded in 1596 using funds left in the will of Frances Sidney, Countess of Sussex, and it was from the start a firmly Protestant institution with a Puritan ethos. However, Cromwell never completed his studies at Cambridge, leaving in 1617 to look after his mother and seven unmarried sisters following the death of his father. From there, he may have received training at Lincoln's Inn in London, one of several legal inns responsible for training England's legal minds for a place in court, but while several of his ancestors had trained there and his son would also do so, no record of Oliver's presence remains at the Inn.

On August 22, 1620 Cromwell married Elizabeth Bourchier, the daughter of a leather merchant and Essex land owner. Over the next 18 years, the couple had nine children: five boys and four girls. Of the boys, one died in infancy and two in early adulthood, and it was the third son, Richard, who would eventually become Cromwell's heir.

Portrait of Cromwell's wife

Portrait of Richard Cromwell

Marriage brought Cromwell into the same social circles as many of London's leading merchants. This was an influential network of successful businessmen, influenced by the political schemes of the Earls of Holland and Warwick. London was the economic and political heart of England, and it held huge influence over the country and its government. The London mob had been known to proclaim kings and lynch politicians, while the city's merchants and craftsmen connected England into the growing global economy. To be a man of influence in London was to be a man of influence on the stage of England.

Still, not everything went smoothly for Cromwell. By 1628, he was suffering from would now be considered depression, which at its worst made daily activities almost unbearable. Still a relatively minor local figure, Cromwell also found himself caught up in a dispute among Huntingdon's gentry about a new charter for the town, and he had to appear before the royal Privy Council as a result. It was probably because of this that he sold most of his Huntingdon property and moved to St. Ives in Cambridgeshire.

Now reduced to the social and economic status of yeoman farmers, Cromwell and his brother Henry kept a smallholding on which they raised sheep and chickens, but in 1636, his fortunes took another turn when he inherited not only various property in Ely but the job of tithe collector for Ely Cathedral from a maternal uncle. Such inherited jobs were common at the time, and some could provide a living for relatively little work. This brought his income back up to its previous level, if not higher, and returned him to the ranks of the gentry.

Cromwell's house in Ely

Cromwell's personal and financial crises of the 1620s and 1630s also brought about a religious transformation in him. Though always Protestant, he had not always been a Puritan, and as late as 1626, he showed signs of a less radical faith, despite his education and family influences. However, in the 1630s, he experienced a religious awakening, coming around to the Puritan perspective of the religious independents. He believed that the Reformation had not gone far enough, that England remained a sinful place, and that Catholic ideas and practices needed to be completely excised from the church. This was about more than the moderate Protestantism espoused by the English bishops; it was about tearing up centuries of tradition and starting afresh.

Cromwell was shifting towards the cause of radical transformation, and he was not the only one.

Chapter 2: The Road to War

"If the remonstrance had been rejected I would have sold all I had the next morning and never have seen England more, and I know there are many other modest men of the same resolution." – Oliver Cromwell, 1641

Thanks to the patronage of powerful friends, Cromwell became a Member of Parliament (MP) in the last three Parliaments of Charles I's reign. He was not a major player in the political maneuvers that eventually led to war, but to understand what followed, it is necessary to understand what happened, and how a new and relatively unimportant MP like Cromwell could fit into the picture.

King Charles I

The relationship between the English monarch and Parliament was an ever-shifting one, as there was no written constitution setting out their relative powers but instead a series of compromises and precedents. Originally a way for the king to gather influential people together, listen to their advice, and persuade them to support his policies, Parliament had turned into an institution with its own distinctive role and traditions. By the early 17th century, it was growing in both significance and confidence, and many MPs believed that they had not just a right but a duty to curb the excesses of the monarch. King Charles I, on the other hand, believed that he was appointed by God and had the right to rule without restriction, even if he found himself unable to do so without Parliament's cooperation.

When Charles inherited the throne in 1625, he was received with suspicion in Parliament. The MPs and Lords who made up the two houses of Parliament were, like the rest of the country, predominantly Protestant, with a growing and vocal Puritan minority. Charles on the other hand was a high church Arminian, who within months of becoming king married Catholic French princess Henrietta Maria at a time when the French king was suppressing Protestants. His favorite advisers included the Arminian Bishop William Laud, who wanted to enforce Catholic-style practices within the church. To an English gentry who saw Catholicism as a foreign threat, this king's agenda was extremely suspect, and his lavish lifestyle appalled the Puritans.

William Laud

The other great source of political division involved the royal finances. Much like the rules of the English church and Parliament, those around taxation had been laid down in confusing and contradictory ways over time rather than clearly set out and agreed upon. Needing money to fund foreign wars, but unable to get the taxes he wanted through Parliament, Charles used forced loans and manipulated precedents to raise funds. This angered the people he was taking money from, as well as many MPs, who found themselves deprived of the political leverage that came with granting taxes.

Things started to come to a head in March 1629 when Parliament refused to provide the king with the taxes he wanted. He closed down Parliament, as was his right, but not before MPs had made resolutions against Catholicism, Arminianism and Charles's schemes to raise money. Nine MPs were arrested on the King's orders, and he ruled without Parliament for the next 11 years.

During those 11 years, tensions grew. Unable to create taxes without Parliament, Charles extended the reach of seldom used laws, selling monopolies and taking back lands that had been given to Scottish nobles, all to fill his own coffers. This created anger and resentment throughout the country. Furthermore, religious tensions were also rising. Charles made Laud into the Archbishop of Canterbury in 1633, leading to attacks on Puritan religious practices. Those who did not confirm to official church doctrine were mutilated and imprisoned, creating martyrs for the independent religious cause.

Charles was King of Scotland as well as England, with the two separate countries having shared a monarch since his father, King James VI of Scotland, inherited the English throne as King James I. But Charles's high-handed approach to politics caused further trouble north of the border, and not just because of the lands he had taken back from the nobility. The Scots were Presbyterian Protestants, and Charles wanted to enforce the same religious practices on them as he supported in England. His attempt to enforce use of the English Book of Common Prayer led to a rebellion by the Scots in 1639, a rebellion which ultimately became known as the Bishops' Wars.

Wars were expensive to fight, and even the measures Charles had used throughout the 1630s could not fund a war to bring the Scots into line. Thus, in 1640, he reluctantly recalled Parliament, his sole purpose being to raise taxes. Cromwell made his second appearance in Parliament as the MP for Ely in this sitting. He was one of many Puritans voted in by electors who were less than enthusiastic about paying for a war to enforce religious practices they themselves opposed. Within a month, it was clear that Charles would not get the taxes he wanted, and Parliament was once again dissolved, earning it the nickname of the Short Parliament.

The King could make the English Parliament go away, but he could not do the same for the Scottish rebellion. Many Scottish soldiers were veterans of the bitter religious fighting in Europe, which was then in the middle of the Thirty Years War. After they beat the English at the Battle of Newburn on 28 August 1640 and occupied northern England, Charles was forced to make a humiliating peace, and then, adding insult to injury, he had to summon Parliament to raise money he had promised to the Scots in return for an end to the war.

This Parliament, which became known as the Long Parliament, first assembled on November 3, 1640. Cromwell was once again in its midst, this time as MP for Cambridge, a position probably gained through political patronage. He had moved with his family to London, where he was part of a Puritan political and religious network. This group, which included various MPs and the Earls of Essex, Warwick and Bedford, had a reforming agenda. They wanted to see regular Parliaments keeping the King in check and a greater degree of religious freedom.

Cromwell was now playing a more important role in politics. In the first week of the new Parliament, he presented a petition for the release from prison of John Lilburne, a famous Puritan agitator. In May 1641 he put forward the Annual Parliaments Bill for its second reading, one of the reformers' attempts to extend their authority through legislation. In the same month he and Henry Vane the Younger introduced one of the most radical proposals yet, the Root and Branch Bill, which sought to abolish the episcopacy and so create a less hierarchical church over which it would be harder for the monarch to assert control.

Though Parliament as a whole was not yet ready for such radical ideas, neither was it ready to give King Charles what he wanted. Of 493 MPs in the Long Parliament, over 350 opposed the king. In return for the funds he so desperately needed, it forced Charles to accept measures that prevented him from dissolving Parliament, as well as the execution of one of his key advisors and other measures loathsome to the monarch.

Charles's main political battleground might be England, but those battles were often triggered by events in the other countries he ruled. In October 1641, Irish Catholics revolted against Protestant English settlers, but while both sides in Parliament wanted to bring the rebels to heel, they argued over the funding and control of the army needed to do the job. More MPs supported Charles in the face of this outside threat, but enough opposed him for him to believe rumors that they planned to impeach his queen.

On January 4, 1642 Charles tried to arrest the leaders of the opposition in the chamber of Parliament. This exposed him as a despot, but also as a failure, since the six men escaped before Charles and his soldiers arrived. Cromwell witnessed firsthand an attempt to persecute the leaders of his political faction, men whose agenda he had supported and whose ideals he shared. Men who in his eyes were only seeking a better future for England.

Following the failed arrests, the country slid ever faster towards polarization and conflict. Charles fled London, which came under the control of Parliament, and both sides started raising armies, even as negotiations took place. Ultimately, there was to be no agreement; on August 22, 1642, Charles raised the royal standard at Nottingham and the First Civil War began.

Chapter 3: The First Civil War

"I had rather have a plain, russet-coated Captain, that knows what he fights for, and loves what he knows, than that you call a Gentleman and is nothing else." – Oliver Cromwell, 1643

The First Civil War, like so many civil conflicts, was fought not just between professionals but between enthusiastic amateurs, men determined to make their mark on the country. Oliver Cromwell was one such man. At the start of the war, Cromwell's only military experience was in the trained bands, local militias raised for purposes of defense, but as a member of the landed gentry, an MP and even a minor player in the politics leading up to the war, he had enough status and money to make an officer of himself. Like other men in similar positions, he raised troops to fight for the Parliamentary cause, in his case a cavalry troop from Cambridgeshire, and went to join the army.

Raising his cavalry troop was perhaps the first time that Cromwell was able to display the leadership skills which would make him so influential. Unlike some other officers, he successfully gathered a large troop of men, not just through his moderate wealth but through his personal influence. Indeed, while nobody could have foreseen it, this marked the beginning of a great military career.

The First Civil War was bitter, devastating and often close fought. Cromwell arrived too late to take part in the Battle of Edgehill, the war's first major engagement, on October 22, 1642, but Edgehill was not the decisive engagement both sides hoped for, and the war quickly spread. Cromwell's troop became a full regiment over the winter of 1642-3, and part of the Eastern Association, an organization of troops from England's eastern counties initially commanded by Baron Grey of Werke. As his title suggests, military leadership was a predominantly noble pursuit even in an armed struggle against the king.

Baron Grey of Werke

As a captain of horse, Cromwell soon started to make a name for himself by helping to prevent royalist advances south. With Hull threatened by the king's men in July, he was one of the officers sent to relieve a parliamentary position in the region. He took Burghley House and relieved the troops at Gainsborough on July 28, 1643 through a decisive and courageous cavalry action, but across the country the royalists were advancing, and without enough infantry to hold his position, Cromwell withdrew south.

Cromwell's capability as a commander led him to rise through the ranks, and when the Earl of Manchester took over the Eastern Association troops in August 1643, Cromwell was appointed Lieutenant General of the Horse. But while he was respected as a commander, he clashed with many of the men around him, including Manchester, due to his egalitarian and strongly Puritan opinions. Not everyone on the Parliamentary side held the same views on the future of England, divisions which would become significant after the war, and a traditionally-minded nobleman like Manchester, whose own position was reliant upon the existing social and political order, was not a good fit with a fire and brimstone Puritan like Cromwell.

From May-July 1644, the Eastern Association besieged the royalists holding Lincoln. Prince Rupert, a leading royalist commander, broke the siege on July 1 and then led his troops out to fight the parliamentary forces on July 2. What followed was the Battle of Marston Moor, in which Cromwell played a decisive part. Despite the success of Cromwell's cavalry on the left flank, the rest of the army almost went into retreat, pushed back by the royalists, but he rallied his battle-weary troops, got around behind the enemy lines and attacked them from the rear. The enemy flank was shattered, and the outnumbered royalists soon surrendered.

Two weeks later, York surrendered, leaving Parliament dominant in the war, but despite this decisive engagement, Parliament failed to capitalize on the victory. Without a strong central organization and leadership, the army failed to properly coordinate, leading to indecisive engagements and the surrender of one of its commanders. In October, King Charles escaped an encircling maneuver at the Second Battle of Newbury, a failure for which Cromwell blamed Manchester, leading to further disputes between the two men.

In the face of these failures, Parliament reformed its forces as the New Model Army, the first English army to be uniformly dressed in their distinctive red coats. These reforms towards a more professional army were embodied in the New Model Ordinance and the Self-Denying Ordinance passed by Parliament in early 1645, which reshaped the army on a national basis rather than leaving its organization to local bodies. The Ordinances also prevented Members of Parliament, whether lords like Manchester or MPs sitting in the House of Commons, from being military commanders, forcing them to choose between political and military power. Such was Cromwell's status that an exception was made for him and he retained both positions, but the rest gave up their military positions. Cromwell would no longer have to work with Manchester.

Cromwell played a leading role in the military reforms, and when the New Model Army set out on campaign in April 1645 he was its cavalry commander and second-in-command, under Sir Thomas Fairfax.

A portrait of Fairfax

Cromwell would now take a vital part in the most decisive battle of the First Civil War. The Battle of Naseby, fought on June 14, 1645, was a critical victory for the New Model Army. Prince Rupert's cavalry broke the parliamentary left flank and then went on to chase down the routed soldiers and attack their baggage train. However, Cromwell, having achieved dominance on the opposite flank, gathered his forces and rallied the broken parliamentary left. He and Fairfax then advanced their cavalry on the royalist infantry from both sides, bringing about a decisive victory and forcing thousands of men to surrender. Cromwell was later quoted as saying before the battle, "I could not, riding out alone about my business, but smile out to God in praises, in assurance of victory because God would, by things that are not, bring to naught things that are." Contemporary English writer John Aubrey referenced Cromwell's seemingly strange antics ahead of this battle and future ones: "One that I knew was at the battle of Dunbar, told me that Oliver was carried on with a Divine impulse; he did laugh so excessively as if he had been drunk; his eyes sparkled with spirits. He obtain'd a great victory; but the action was said to be contrary to human prudence. The same fit of laughter seized Oliver Cromwell just before the battle of Naseby; as a kinsman of mine, and a great favourite of his, Colonel J. P. then present, testified. Cardinal Mazerine said, that he was a lucky fool."

Although the war would run on for another year, it now became a mopping up operation. The

New Model Army had more men, better supplies, and higher morale, as well as the strategic advantage. They besieged and captured royalist strongholds, chased the royalists around the country, and undermined Charles's military support. He eventually handed himself over to the Scots, who had played their own independent part in the Civil War, often on the parliamentary side. The last substantial royalist stronghold of Oxford surrendered in June 1646. The fighting was not entirely over - Harlech in Wales held out as a royalist bastion until March 1647 - but the King had surrendered and the matter was decided.

Cromwell's impact on the war, and thus his future political standing, was based on his superiority as a cavalry commander. Like so many others in the war, he started out as an amateur, but he was a gifted one. Charismatic and determined, he was able to recruit more men than many other cavalry commanders and to keep them in order on the battlefield. Rather than the wild pursuits of Prince Rupert, which used the fury and momentum of a successful cavalry charge to run the routed enemy into the ground, Cromwell brought his men back into order after a success. This meant that they were more useful on the battlefield, not just chasing away enemies in skirmishes on the flanks but turning that advantage into superior numbers and flanking maneuvers on the enemy's infantry lines. Cromwell also changed the way that his men fought, using close order cavalry formations to give his charges more impact. The role of cavalry on the battlefield was changing across Europe at the time, and in Cromwell, Parliament was lucky to have a commander who adapted well to the changing face of war.

Over four bloody years, Oliver Cromwell had risen from a minor opposition politician into a leading figure of the national army. He and his ideological allies now controlled a country damaged by the divisions and devastation of war, but there was a peace to be built, and that would prove an equally difficult task.

Chapter 4: A Failed Peace

"We declared our intentions to preserve monarchy, and they still are so, unless necessity enforce an alteration. It's granted the king has broken his trust, yet you are fearful to declare you will make no further addresses... look on the people you represent, and break not your trust, and expose not the honest party of your kingdom, who have bled for you, and suffer not misery to fall upon them for want of courage and resolution in you, else the honest people may take such courses as nature dictates to them." – Oliver Cromwell, 1648

Even after the First Civil War ended, the divisions were complex and the sides shifted over time, but they can be boiled down to two main viewpoints. On one side of the parliamentary movement were those who sought moderate levels of reform in order to lower the risk of a despotic king and a Catholic-influenced church. Dominant in Parliament, their preference was for reconciliation with Charles. Including many of the men who had led the country towards war, as well as those who had more reluctantly taken Parliament's side, they tried to put together a settlement in which everybody had a part. Charles would be restored while accepting certain constraints. The established Church of England would be replaced by a Presbyterian model like the Scottish church, a form of Protestantism in which the church was run by a body of elders rather than dictated to by a single leading figure.

On the other side were the radicals, men who held less sway in Parliament but were hugely influential in the New Model Army, where they often provided a voice for ordinary soldiers. Several different Protestant sects had emerged during the chaos of the First Civil War, when no one was able to undertake the traditional governmental duty of suppressing religious dissent. They combined radical political and religious views, these being one and the same in the 17th century mindset. Most eloquent and coherent were groups such as the Levellers and the Diggers, who pushed for levels of political and economic equality that were unthinkable to traditionalists. They sought religious freedom for Protestants so that they themselves could continue to worship as they saw fit, and opposed the imposition of a nationally aligned church, even a Presbyterian one.

These divisions were not purely ideological either. Many moderates wanted to disband the New Model Army now that the war was won, and this had practical consequences for the soldiers. They were still owed pay for having taken part in the risky business of war, and the army had provided them with a voice for the first time in their lives. An attack on the army was therefore also an attack on their interests.

Hanging over this were the specters of Catholicism and Scotland. Even the most radical Puritans did not want to see toleration extended to Catholics, though some in the country still secretly leaned that way. Meanwhile, the Scots, themselves armed and organized and theoretically subjects of the same king, were eager for a settlement that would favor their own political and religious interests.

Cromwell's sympathies lay more with the radicals of the New Model Army. These were his men, the ones who had fought and bled at his command, and they shared his Puritan faith and his distaste for anything with even a hint of Popery about it. At the same time, he was not an extreme hardliner; he was a member of the landed gentry and not interested in the radical social transformation sought by the Levellers.

Parliament's intention to disband the army with its wages unpaid led to a mutiny, during which the regiments elected Agitators to voice their concerns. Most of the officers, including Cromwell, sided with the mutineers. They seized the King, who at that time was held by Parliament, took control of London, and published a manifesto of their grievances and desired reforms. Cromwell had his son-in-law Henry Ireton put together a proposed package of reforms, the *Head of Proposals*. This aimed for a constitutional monarchy involving religious toleration, regular but reformed Parliaments, reduced power for bishops, and measures intended to prevent the King immediately rolling back the reforms.

Ireton

At the same time, there were many radical agitators in the army, men pushing for a more substantial change in the country than most MPs and the gentry officers of the New Model Army would ever endorse. These proposals were presented in two successive documents, *The Case of the Armie Truly Stated* and its successor *The Agreement of the People*. The radicals wanted more than just to use Parliament to curb the King. Having fought and bled for Parliament, they now wanted to be represented within it, with equal representation for all men in Parliament, rather than the existing system which only gave votes to a wealthy minority.

The Putney Debates, a series of meetings between army officers and representatives of the common soldiers, took place in October and early November 1647 with the aim of finding common ground between these two approaches to reform, both radical by the standards of the era and yet somehow at odds with each other. Cromwell took a leading part in these debates, chairing meetings, supporting the *Head of Proposals* and trying to achieve reconciliation. He used prayer as a way of creating bonds between men with very different views but a shared and fervent Protestant faith. In line with his own beliefs, he also encouraged all involved to seek guidance from God in their prayers. It was indicative of the challenge he faced that these men, who shared his strong faith in a personal relationship with the divine, could return to the meetings after a night of prayer with their opposing beliefs reinforced rather than reconciled. This radicalism showed no signs of abating with its flames fanned by agitators from outside the army, and Cromwell and Fairfax eventually came to see it as a form of mutiny. They gathered the army in a series of separate mass meetings, used force of will to achieve unity in place of divisive radicalism, and court-martialed nine leading mutineers.

Though he was a reformer and has gone down in history as the man who led the forces of representation against an authoritarian monarch, it would be a mistake to view Cromwell as a democrat in the modern sense. As the Putney Debates showed, he was a man with a deep sense of right and wrong, and one who was only so willing to listen to dissenting voices. He despised the tyranny he associated with Charles, but he did not see all men as equally worthy of participation in the business of running the country. He wanted leadership by a group of God-fearing, property-owning men who shared his Protestant convictions and who were as uncomfortable with the unruly mob as with an untrustworthy monarch. While radicals sought to do away with Charles, Cromwell sought a way to achieve a stable reconciliation with the King, though on more radical terms than those favored by his parliamentary colleagues.

It is a sign of just how badly King Charles misjudged his position that he went from this point, when Cromwell would execute his own men rather than end negotiations with the King, to a situation in which Cromwell played a leading part in having him executed. However, Charles was a schemer and a man who, against all evidence, seemed unable to recognize that events might not go his way. With Parliament and the New Model Army fractured on the question of where to take the peace, he played the two off against each other, all the while negotiating with a third party: the Scots. While the Putney debates were still ongoing, Charles escaped captivity and tried to flee to France. But the governor of the Isle of White, who Charles believed would assist him, instead imprisoned the King, and he found himself once again a captive of Parliament.

Unable to escape the country, he instead entered into a secret treaty with the Scots in December 1647. His new allies agreed to invade England in support of a royalist uprising the following year. This agreement was not made public until it was discussed in the Scottish Parliament in February, but it was clear to politicians in England that the king could not be trusted and that violence was once again impending. Defenses were prepared, and in February 1648 Parliament agreed by a majority of 80-50 on the Vote of No Addresses, a public declaration that they would no longer negotiate with the king. In doing this, and in justifying its position, Parliament arranged for pamphlets to be printed explaining and condemning Charles's duplicitous behavior, as well as listing the king's previous misdeeds. This turned public opinion further towards the radicals, galvanizing the country not just for war but for the changes that would follow it.

During the interim period between the two civil wars, the peace had seen Cromwell's position strengthened. He was the officers' prime mover in the Putney Debates and showed the common soldier that he would listen to their concerns, but that he would bring them into line if needed. Meanwhile his opponents were rushing down paths that would see them critically weakened. Charles wasted his opportunity for reconciliation under a constitutional monarchy, while Parliament failed in its dealings with him. As the country once again headed down a polarizing path towards violence, Oliver Cromwell was looking stronger than ever.

Chapter 5: The Second Civil War

"No one rises so high as he who knows not whither he is going." – Oliver Cromwell

The willingness of the Scots to support Charles I in the Second Civil War, despite their previous alliance with Parliament, was motivated in part by what they saw of England's sectarian divisions and in part by what Charles himself had to offer. Despite the efforts of Cromwell and his allies to achieve unity, England had been torn apart ideologically during the first war, unleashing a wave of radical sects pulling the country in different directions. The Scottish nobility feared facing this sort of chaos in their own country, and they also worried that without the threat of the Royalist cause, the New Model Army might bring its disciplined troops and its religion north of the border in a new invasion. Charles played to these fears, holding out an alternative that conceded just enough to bridge the gap between an Arminian king and a Presbyterian country. In return for their support Charles would acknowledge the Scottish church as it stood and bring in Presbyterianism in England, though temporarily at first.

Meanwhile, the Puritanism of Cromwell and his colleagues was causing discontent, which also gave the royalists hope. In an attempt to stamp out anything that smelled even faintly of Catholicism and to impose serious, virtuous behavior on an unruly population, major holidays had been banned. Phallic looking Maypoles, drunken St George's Day revelries, celebrations of the King's accession to the throne, and other similar events were abolished. But the most serious blow was the banning of Christmas festivities, including decorations and days off work. Deprived of their opportunity for good cheer in the darkest part of the year, people rioted all across the country, most seriously in Kent. There violent protest turned into an armed rebellion.

The Second Civil War opened with terrible inevitability in late April 1648, with the occupation of Berwick and Carlisle in northern England by men gathered to fight for Charles's cause. In the southeast, men of Essex and Kent continued to defy Parliament, while south Wales, which had held out to the bitter end of the previous war, once more rose up for the king. Fairfax was sent to deal with the southeastern counties, eventually containing the rebels in Colchester, while risings in the southwest faltered. The duty of dealing with Wales was given to Cromwell.

Since its conquest by the English in the 13th century, Wales had been controlled by a serious of castles dominating towns along the coastline. Regaining control of the region was therefore a matter of retaking these castles. Though Cromwell's skills as a cavalry commander were unlikely to play a major role in this, he was by now recognized as a leading general and hence put in charge of the army that marched west.

As it turned out, the Welsh campaign was a short and successful one for Cromwell and one in which he proved less merciful than in the previous war. He captured Chepstow and Tenby in late May, burned down Carmarthen Castle, and moved on to besiege Pembroke Castle, the heart of the revolt. Isolated and faced with the might of the New Model Army, the castle surrendered on July 11, 1648. Cromwell was lenient towards longstanding royalists among the rebels but not towards those who had defected from the parliamentary side, and one of their leaders was eventually executed in London.

It took the Scots a couple of months to mobilize their army, so they didn't invade England until July 8. By then, royalists had seized Pontefract Castle and the Scarborough garrison had defected to the King, giving the rebels four strongholds in northern England. Aside from that, however, the country failed to rise up in revolt as Charles had hoped. A naval mutiny had been contained, the rebels in the southeast were cornered by Fairfax, and those in Wales were falling to Cromwell.

After capturing Pembroke, Cromwell took 4,000 of his men and marched north to face the Scots. He met with another small parliamentary army under John Lambert, with Cromwell taking overall command, and on August 17, they caught up with the larger Scottish army under the Duke of Hamilton, which was strung out along its route of march south, and defeated them in battle at Preston. Cromwell pressed hard against the retreating Scots and royalists, pursuing them relentlessly over the next week until the infantry had all been killed or surrendered and Hamilton had fled with the remnants of his cavalry.

The Battle of Preston ended any hopes of a royalist victory, but Colchester held out under siege throughout the summer. Civilians suffered from starvation, and the town was devastated by artillery bombardments. Both sides blamed each other for the horrors inflicted there and feared that England was slipping into the sort of brutality seen in the religious conflict of the Thirty Years War, then reaching its end on the continent.

If the rest of the country was polarized by the propaganda and politics leading up to the Second Civil War, Cromwell's views became polarized by the war itself. He came to agree with the radical preachers who blamed King Charles for the nation's woes. His was a politics built on faith, and he believed that the army's success showed that both King Charles and Parliament, which kept seeking compromise with the monarch, lacked real authority from God. Thus, there was now no doubt in Cromwell's mind that there could be no peace through compromise with Charles, and if Parliament could not realize this in its own wisdom, then it would fall to the army, blessed by God and led by righteous men like Cromwell and Ireton, to set them straight.

The Civil Wars were over, but the struggle for the future was not.

Chapter 6: The Commonwealth

"I tell you we will cut off his head with the crown upon it." – Oliver Cromwell, 1648

"I am persuaded that this is a righteous judgment of God upon these barbarous wretches, who have imbrued their hands in so much innocent blood and that it will tend to prevent the effusion of blood for the future, which are satisfactory grounds for such actions, which otherwise cannot but work remorse and regret." – Oliver Cromwell after the Siege of Drogheda, 1649

The fallout from the Second Civil War left Parliament in an awkward position. As a body it had previously made clear its unwillingness to depose Charles I, but the lead up to the second war had included a public declaration that it would no longer negotiate with the king. While many were unwilling to deal any longer with the scheming monarch, the majority of MPs also feared radical change, given its potential for social and political disruption. Even the arguments for launching the first war had centered around defending the traditional rights of Parliament and the propertied classes against the King's allegedly unprecedented and illegal tyranny, not a radical agenda of curbing royal power. However, while the majority of MPs were ready to repeal the Vote of No Addresses and return to negotiations with Charles, those who opposed negotiation were both larger in number and firmer in their convictions than ever before.

Among them was Cromwell. Parliament sent representatives to talk with the king at Newport, and by November they were on the verge of an agreement, with Charles's determined attachment to the power of bishops the only significant issue still in the way. But as in the period before the Second Civil War, the New Model Army's leaders and soldiers were more radical than Parliament. Even the officers in charge, conservative as they were compared with the Leveller agitators, were unhappy at the idea of retaining Charles as monarch. The division within the army was now over how to respond, with a group around Fairfax feeling that it was not the army's place to interfere in Parliament's business, while a group around Cromwell's son-in-law Ireton believed that they had a moral duty to prevent Charles returning to power. While heated debates took place in London, Cromwell stayed in the north with his army, avoiding having to take a side.

Parliament delayed discussing the Remonstrance, a document of Ireton's creation that set out the army's view that Charles should be tried as a criminal rather than negotiated with as a monarch. This delay finally pushed Fairfax into moving against Parliament in December 1648. He set firmer guards around Charles, ordered Cromwell to return to London, and mustered the army. Persuaded by friendly MPs not to completely dissolve Parliament, the army instead sent Colonel Thomas Pride to exclude moderates from Parliament on December 6-12, an event known as Pride's Purge. What remained - 200 MPs out of what had been 471 - is remembered as the Rump Parliament.

Ironically, it seems that Cromwell, though convinced of the need to get rid of Charles, hoped that he could be persuaded to abdicate in favor of his third son, Henry Duke of Gloucester, seen as less of an absolutist than his father. However, Charles would not consider this, and by Christmas Cromwell reluctantly accepted that a more radical approach was needed. Thus, on January 1, 1649, with encouragement from Cromwell, the Rump Parliament agreed to set up a High Court of Justice to try Charles for treason. Many people, Charles included, refused to cooperate with a trial whose legal standing was extremely questionable, but this great display still went ahead, starting on January 20 and ending on January 27, when the king was sentenced to death. Cromwell, Ireton and Pride were among the men who signed the death warrant. The king was executed on January 30, 1649, but it took two more months to decide who or what would take his place. The result was the declaration of the Commonwealth of England, a republic governed by the Rump Parliament and a smaller Council of State, which filled the executive role previously held by the king and royal council. Cromwell was a member of both bodies.

A depiction of the trial of King Charles I

An illustration depicting Cromwell leading the imprisonment of Charles I

Paul Delaroche's painting of Cromwell and the corpse of Charles I

Fairfax, who did not support the trial and execution of Charles, was withdrawing from public affairs, leaving Cromwell as the unchallenged leader of the army. His first task was to deal with Ireland, where royalists were gathering the support of Catholic rebels. However, in April 1649, as Cromwell was selecting the regiments to take with him, Levellers in the army started to protest against Parliament and the military leaders, who they saw as not radical enough in their agenda. This was meant to become a general uprising in May, and though it was never as successful as the organizers hoped, Cromwell and Fairfax had to lead forces into western England to put down the revolt. Along the way, they made promises to the rebels that they would dissolve the Rump and hold new elections, but these promises were never kept. In the end, the rebellion was not ended by negotiation but through a brief and bloody skirmish in mid-May which effectively ended the Leveller influence on politics.

Parliament had wanted to re-conquer Ireland since it rebelled in 1641, and Cromwell viewed the Irish rebels as a serious menace, both because of the deaths of many Protestants during previous revolts and because of their Catholicism, which he saw as a pernicious foreign influence and a deviation from true Christian faith. He arrived in Ireland in August 1649, shortly after the main rebel army had been defeated by another force. What remained was to besiege and capture rebel settlements, a task which he started on the east coast with the town of Drogheda. Though hugely outnumbered, the garrison in Drogheda refused to surrender. Cromwell responded with a bombardment on September 10 and an assault the next day, pushing into the town. When the garrison still refused to surrender, as it would normally have been expected to do, Cromwell ordered that anyone found with arms should be executed, not captured. The cornered soldiers were massacred, as were priests and some civilians, and though Cromwell never ordered the deaths of civilians, he later conceded, "I believe we put to the sword the whole number of the defendants. I do not think thirty of the whole number escaped with their lives…in the heat of the action, I forbade them to spare any that were in arms in the town".

Similar carnage took place when he captured Wexford the following month, after which New Ross surrendered rather than resist and face a massacre, but Waterford, which Cromwell besieged in November, held out. Cromwell eventually had to give up on this siege as his army suffered from winter diseases and poor weather, but by January 1650, Cromwell was back in the field, besieging and assaulting castles. He captured the rebel capital of Kilkenny on March 27, and the ineptitude of his opponents then led a large portion of the rebels to defect back to Parliament. The last substantial rebel stronghold was Clonmel, where thousands of New Model Army soldiers died due to a trap set by the garrison commander, but it ultimately capitulated in May.

By now, news had arrived that Charles I's son, the future Charles II, had signed an alliance with the Scots, so Cromwell left Ireton to mop up the Irish rebels and returned to England to face this new northern menace. That June, Parliament made Fairfax the official commander of the defense of northern England, with Cromwell once again as his second-in-command, but they also gave the order that this defense should take the form of a preemptive invasion of Scotland, and on June 22, Fairfax resigned rather than lead an invasion which he did not agree with. Cromwell could not dissuade him, so on June 28, the former cavalry commander was appointed as Lord General.

Charles II

Now in overall command of the New Model Army, Cromwell marched his troops north. The need to deal with Ireland and prevent rebellions in England meant that the Scottish invasion army was constantly low on supplies, suffering from disease and malnutrition, and they initially struggled with a strong Scottish defensive line. Besieged by the numerically superior Scots at Dunbar, Cromwell ordered a night attack, even though most of his commanders advised him to withdraw. By exploiting a weakness in the Scottish line, he was able to outmaneuver his opponents, achieving a crushing victory in which 4,000 Scottish soldiers were killed and 10,000 captured.

A painting depicting Cromwell at Dunbar

Cromwell went on to conquer Edinburgh, where he showed far more mercy than he had in Ireland. He wanted to dislodge the Scottish leaders who had pushed for war and integrate Scotland peacefully into English territory, so massacres were out of the question. Instead, he launched a two-pronged assault into western Scotland in November, in which the Scottish army was smashed by English commander John Lambert. An attempt to seize the Fife in February 1651 ended in failure for Cromwell and he became seriously sick, but his opponents were too divided to make the most of the Lord General's convalescence.

Following further successes for Cromwell and Lambert in June and July, Cromwell deliberately left the way open for Charles to invade England. Charles rose to the bait, after which he was pursued by Cromwell and most of his troops. English cavalry harassed the Scots on their way south, a reminder of the devastating pursuit of the last Scottish invasion. Charles tried to rally royalists at Worcester, but few flocked to his banner and he was thoroughly defeated by Cromwell. Almost the entire army surrendered, with Charles himself one of the very few to escape.

With the Civil Wars over, Cromwell encouraged the Rump Parliament to follow his reforming agenda and create a new constitution to fill the gap left by the king. He wanted to see the countries of England (including long-conquered Wales), Scotland and Ireland brought together in a single political body with a national church that tolerated different Protestant observances, and he wanted fresh parliamentary elections. However, while it introduced some religious toleration, the Rump failed to bring about substantial reforms such as replacing existing church tithes, and did not set a date for the election that would see it replaced. It also angered many men in the army by ordering the seizure of royalist estates; though the army had fought hard against the royalists, it had also encouraged their surrender by promising not to seize these lands, so Parliament's actions undermined the honor and intentions of the army.

Though both the army and the Rump were divided, the gap between the two bodies was greater, and army officers started encouraging Cromwell to step in and deal with Parliament's failings. On April 18-19, 1653, he met with his officers and parliamentary allies, creating a proposal for Parliament to replace itself with a temporary governing body of forty men. However, on April 20, news arrived that Parliament, rather than debate this proposal, was debating its own different bill. Cromwell went to Parliament, took his seat, listened to the debate as long as he could tolerate, and then rose to his feet. He gave an angry speech against the failings of the Rump, called in soldiers, and dispersed Parliament.

After that, Cromwell convened a new Council of State, whose purpose was to set up a new body to govern the country. This Nominated Assembly consisted of men chosen by the army for their righteous religious beliefs, fitting Cromwell's views that the country should be run by the godly, and it first met on July 4. He gave the Assembly until November 1654 to establish a body to replace itself, which would in turn produce a permanent constitution. However, the Nominated Assembly, popularly known as the Barebones Parliament after one of its most radical members, was sharply divided between radical and moderate reformers who could agree on absolutely nothing. By November, it was clear that the assembly was not working, and on December 12, the moderates resigned in bunches, brought in soldiers to prevent the remaining assembly from sitting, and went to Cromwell asking him to replace the assembly with a new constitution. Two parliaments had now failed in the space of a single year, and a different form of leadership was needed.

That form would be Cromwell.

Chapter 7: Lord Protector

Mid-17th century portrait of Cromwell

"That which brought me into the capacity I now stand in, was the Petition and Advice given me by you, who, in reference to the ancient Constitution, did draw me here to accept the place of Protector. There is not a man living can say I sought it, no not a man, nor woman, treading upon English ground." – Oliver Cromwell

On two occasions, Cromwell had tried to create a collective body to make decisions, only to see it dissolved at gunpoint, so he now accepted what he had so long resisted: a country run by one man, that man being him. On December 15, the Instrument of Government, a constitution drafted by John Lambert, was adopted. The Instrument was based on the principle that power needed to be balanced between different bodies to prevent despotism, whether by a sole ruler or a corrupt assembly, but Lambert also recognized that assemblies and parliaments could not act quickly and decisively, and that such decisiveness was sometimes needed. Thus, three branches of government were set up : a large legislative Parliament, a small executive Council, and a Lord Protector who oversaw and was limited by both. Parliament was reformed in the process, and both Catholics and Royalists were excluded to prevent a new Parliament that would vote the monarchy back in.

John Lambert

On December 16, 1653, under the provisions of the Instrument, Cromwell was sworn in as Lord Protector of the Commonwealth of England, Scotland and Ireland. The title of Lord Protector had previously been used by those acting as regents in the absence of a monarch, but now it became the title for the man permanently replacing the king. Though he wore his familiar plain black clothes rather than grandiose royal regalia for the swearing in ceremony, what followed had the familiar governmental form of a monarchy. Cromwell could call and dissolve Parliament, received a very large income from the nation, and continued to control his ever-loyal army. He could veto laws, though this power was limited, and he ran the Council. Church bells were rung following his investiture, and he was even being spoken to as "Your Highness."

One of the most significant novelties of Cromwell's regime was that he was the first English ruler to have a permanent standing army. The New Model Army, as a reformed and professional body, had replaced local militias and armies raised on the basis of need. It was fiercely attached to Cromwell, who had led it through war, reform and spectacular victories. This gave him greater power in practice even than that given to him by the new constitution.

The most urgent issue to be addressed was making peace with the Dutch. A war had recently broken out over control of trade, a war in which Cromwell played no part because it was fought at sea, but both sides were tiring of the war, and in April 1654 peace was made, a goal in which Parliament's negotiators had previously failed. In developing diplomatic relations with other countries, the Lord Protector adopted the pomp and circumstance of formal receptions for ambassadors, something abandoned since Charles's fall. This was done to meet the expectations of these visitors and assert English authority, but it also reinforced Cromwell's position as a proxy king. Whether such grandeur was needed is questionable since other European states, very aware of the military power with which Cromwell had laid waste to the ambitions of Charles, Ireland, and Scotland, all rushed to establish good relations with England's new ruler.

Since Cromwell's return to London as a general in 1650, he and his family had been living in accommodation attached to the Palace of Whitehall. The Palace itself was now given to them as their home, setting them up in the sort of grandeur expected of a head of state. They were given a household of servants and entertainers, many of whom had previously served the king, and the staffing of the Protector's household increasingly came to resemble a royal one. Half a dozen other royal residences, including Windsor Castle, were also made available to him.

In keeping with his Puritan character, Cromwell accepted these monarchical trappings as a necessary part of maintaining the authority of the head of state, rather than seeking out such extreme privilege. Some saw this as Cromwell putting on a show of humility, but he was a deeply religious man, wedded to a more egalitarian faith than that of Charles I. If he had really wanted such status and grandeur, it would have been his for the taking years before, given the power he wielded in the country. The fact was that, culturally as well as politically, England and the other nations it had conquered were not ready to do without a single central leader of great authority and status. Despite the protestations of the Levellers and other radicals, Charles's execution left a void, and Cromwell was brought in to fill it.

Cromwell and the Council sought peace at home as well as abroad by trying to unify their previously separate countries. National Parliaments were replaced by Scottish and Irish seats in what had previously been the English Parliament, and other measures were taken to reconcile their people.

In these ways, the new government set about trying to return the country to some kind of stability after the terrible upheavals of the Civil Wars, a policy Cromwell labeled "healing and settling." He rejected the revolutionary social and political reforms favored by Parliamentary radicals and the more extreme religious groups, but in this regard, he faced a struggle with Parliament, which met in its new form for the first time in September 1654. It almost immediately set about challenging the authority of the military-led government and preparing a new constitution. This was not the acquiescent body that Cromwell had looked for after the closure of the last two Parliaments, so he dissolved it in January 1655.

With that action, the tripartite political balance of the Instrument of Government was falling apart, and a failed royalist uprising in March 1655 gave Cromwell an excuse to re-examine the way that the country was governed. Influenced once again by Lambert, the Protectorate's great political philosopher, Cromwell divided England up into 15 military districts. These were governed by Army Major Generals, responsible for maintaining troops, raising taxes and ensuring support for the government. The Major Generals also pushed Cromwell's agenda of Puritan religious reform, with the assistance of commissioners in each county. This system of devolved military dictatorship lasted less than a year, being voted out by a later Parliament, but its short lived activities reopened old wounds and stirred up opposition to the new regime, opposition which would eventually turn into support for the restored monarchy.

Despite his outspoken opposition to both public Catholicism and religious reform more radical than his own, Cromwell believed in freedom of conscience in private worship, and he acted to make this a reality. Hoping to tap into their wealth, he encouraged Jews to return to England after many of them had fled the intolerance of previous regimes. Given his hope for a reformed religious community, Cromwell believed that the Jews would eventually turn to Christianity, but he did not try to enforce this, and compared with much of England's previous history, this was a tolerant period for them.

That said, while he accepted religious freedom in private, Cromwell did not want to see it enacted in public. Puritan moral reforms continued, such as the banning of pagan-looking Christmas festivals that had so recently led to riot and revolt. Where moral character was concerned, Cromwell's pragmatism would only stretch so far.

This approach to religious reform is indicative of the problem at the heart of Cromwell's religious and political thinking, a problem he faced at every turn. A man of deeply held convictions, he believed that a more egalitarian church and state, in which more people were able to participate, was the best bulwark against both political and religious tyranny. Indeed, such egalitarianism was needed in order to give people the freedom to behave in a more godly and upstanding fashion, free from the corrupting influence of bishops and decadent royals. But once they were given that freedom and participation, people failed to live up to the standards Cromwell looked for in them. They embraced frivolousness and drunkenness on public holidays, and they elected radicals and royalists. Instead of becoming good Puritans, they turned against the principles which, in Cromwell's eyes, would set them free.

It was this problem that led Cromwell to become Lord Protector, and that led to solutions such as local government by Major Generals. If people would not do right by choice, then he was willing, when pushed, to lead them to it, but even Cromwell, who had risen from obscurity through his strength of personality, could not make the horse drink. This was shown when Parliament once again met in September 1656. By now, England was at war with Spain, its traditional Catholic enemy, and Cromwell and his advisers hoped that this shared external threat would win Parliament around to their side. Nonetheless, while MPs voted in new funds to fight the war, they also ended the authority of the Major Generals and undermined the policy of religious toleration by persecuting the Quaker James Nayler.

A depiction of Nayler with a "B" branded onto his forehead for blasphemy

This is not to say that Cromwell lacked support in this Parliament, support he had guaranteed by excluding a hundred of the most disruptive members from the moment it first sat. There had long been rumors that he would be made king, and this issue was openly discussed in Parliament in January 1657. The House eventually voted by 123-62 to offer him the crown, and on March 31, this request was made official, but the Humble Petition and Advice did not just ask Cromwell to become king; it also asked him to restore a constitution similar to that which existed before the Instrument of Government. Many people supported this change, given its potential to reduce Cromwell's dominance of Parliament while restoring the comforting familiarity of monarchy, but many also opposed it, including radicals outraged at the idea of restoring the monarchy. Unsurprisingly John Lambert, the author of the Instrument of Government, opposed the dissolution of the settlement he had crafted, and the Humble Petition and Advice marked the end of his period of great influence.

Cromwell himself was deeply divided, torn again by circumstances which put his own principles in conflict. He recognized Parliament as expressing the will of the people, and the importance of listening to this will. He also recognized the practical value of a grand head of state. But he also believed that God had led him to destroy the monarchy, and he could not in good conscience go against this. Thus, after six weeks of wrestling with his conscience and debating with other worthies, Cromwell accepted most of the proposals set out in the Humble Petition, but the one that he rejected was the one which everyone had been talking from the moment he became Lord Protector: the title of king.

A satirical cartoon depicting the Lord Protector usurping the power of kings

On June 26, 1657, Cromwell was given a new public investiture as Lord Protector, one as grand as any coronation ceremony, and those seeking the stability of monarchy now seemed to have what they wanted: a king in all but name. He created hereditary peers, had coins made bearing his image and sought out noble husbands for his daughters. Cromwell had solved his crisis of conscience by disassociating the nature of kingship from its title, thereby rejecting the latter while accepting the former.

A 1658 coin depicting the Lord Protector

When Parliament reconvened in January 1658, it was in its new form, but one which was remarkably similar to the old form from before the Protectorate. Two Houses were once more in place: the Lords, referred to at this time as the "Other House," and the Commons. There was no interference in the election of MPs to the Commons, and thus the troublemakers excluded from the previous Parliament once again took their seats. Once again, however, these republican radicals immediately set about challenging the shape of the new constitution, beginning with the title and authority of the Other House. The ensuing dispute prevented any work getting done and threatened yet more political upheaval, so on February 4, after just 10 days, Cromwell dissolved yet another Parliament.

Chapter 8: Death and Succession

An unfinished portrait of Cromwell by Samuel Cooper

"I desire not to keep my place in this government an hour longer than I may preserve England in its just rights, and may protect the people of God in such a just liberty of their consciences." – Oliver Cromwell

1658 was a period of tragedy for Cromwell. Several close family members died, including his daughter Elizabeth in August. Already ill himself, he personally tended to Elizabeth as she lay dying, and he was devastated by the loss. But the worst was yet to come, for within a month, the Lord Protector himself would be dead.

By the summer of 1658, Cromwell was an increasingly sickly man, suffering from urinary or kidney complaints and a bought of malaria. The struggles to maintain a functioning government cannot have helped his health, and the death of his daughter Elizabeth capped his decline. He died on September 3, 1658, most likely from a bout of septicemia following a urinary infection. The date of his death was also the anniversary of two of his great successes: the battles of Dunbar and Worcester. Cromwell was buried at Westminster Abbey, and if that was not royal enough for the republican ruler, the ceremony was based on that used for King James I.

Chris Nyborg's picture of Cromwell's death mask at Warwick Castle

It is not clear who Cromwell intended to follow him as Lord Protector, and the issue was disputed both by contemporaries and by historians. He may have had his son-in-law Charles Fleetwood in mind, he may have intended through his inaction to nominate no one to follow him, or he may have been preparing his son Richard for the role. Regardless, those around him immediately leapt at the solution that best fit the proxy monarchy of the protectorate by making Richard Cromwell the Lord Protector.

Richard was the third of Oliver and Elizabeth Cromwell's four sons, but by the time of Oliver's death, he was the eldest surviving son. Aside from family connections, however, he was nothing like his the man he succeeded. He lacked his father's political and military inclinations, did not fight in the Civil Wars (though his older brother Oliver was a parliamentary officer and died of typhoid fever while serving in the army), and his political activity was mostly limited to his home county of Hampshire, where he was a Justice of the Peace and took part in local committees. National political influence could have been his for the taking - his younger brother Henry became an MP in 1653 - but he instead retained a more humble station until the first and second Protectorate Parliaments, in which he sat as an MP.

Nonetheless, following the reforms of the Humble Petition, Oliver had involved Richard more in politics. He attended the second investiture ceremony in June 1657, was appointed Chancellor of Oxford University in July, and joined the Council of State in December. Accepting the Humble Petition had made Cromwell responsible for selecting his successor, and he was at least testing Richard's potential for the role.

It is therefore not surprising that Richard found himself as Lord Protector after Oliver's death, but it is also not surprising to find that this humble man lacked the character to hold together a government of uncertain rules and questionable legitimacy, as his father had done since the Civil Wars. Parliament was recalled to deal with the government's debts and met in January 1659, and once again, disputes immediately broke out between moderate Presbyterians, radical reformers and closet royalists. Parliament also fell out with the New Model Army, which felt it was not being paid enough respect and feared that Parliament might disband it to avoid further costs. In April, military officers petitioned the Lord Protector for higher taxation to cover army expenses. They had no respect for Richard, who lacked his father's military background, and were now playing their own game, but Parliament ignored the petition and, remembering the army's interventions to exclude members from Parliament and dissolve previous meetings, passed resolutions to limit meetings by army officers and force them all to swear an oath not to subvert Parliament.

To this, the army responded in predictable fashion, assembling in London and forcing the unhappy Richard Cromwell to dissolve the current Parliament and recall the pro-army Rump Parliament. However, this was as far as cooperation between Richard and the army would ever go; the officers agreed to pay off his debts and provide him with a pension, in return for which he resigned as Lord Protector on May 25, 1659. He lived abroad for most of the next 20 years before returning to live in obscurity in England until his death on July 12, 1712.

What followed was the collapse of everything that Oliver Cromwell had struggled for over the last two decades. The army, Parliament and the citizens of London grappled with each other for control of the country, and even the army no longer remained a united political force. Civil war almost broke out again as a force under Lambert failed to prevent General Monck, the military governor of Scotland, from marching south and dissolving the Rump Parliament. Excluded MPs were restored on condition that they themselves dissolve Parliament, and following fresh elections without military intervention, a new Parliament met on April 25, 1660. Dominated by Presbyterians and Royalists, it accepted a settlement offered by the man titling himself Charles

II, the son and heir of Charles I. On May 25, 1660, Charles II returned to England, and less than two years after Cromwell's death, his work was undone with the restoration of the monarchy.

Chapter 9: Cromwell's Legacy

"During a great part of the eighteenth century most Tories hated him because he overthrew the monarchy, most Whigs because he overthrew Parliament. Since Carlyle wrote, all liberals have seen in him their champion, and all revolutionists have apotheosized the first great representatives of their school; while, on the other side, their opponents have hailed the dictator who put down anarchy. Unless the socialists or the anarchists finally prevail — and perhaps even then — his fame seems as secure as human reputation is likely to be in a changing world." - W.C. Abbott

A statue of Cromwell outside the Palace of Westminster

Cromwell's story is one of the most extraordinary in English history. At his lowest ebb, he was struggling with the emotional darkness of depression, defeated in the petty realm of local politics, and found much of his little wealth gone. Two decades later, he was the ruler of England, feared and respected throughout Europe, and living in a palace while his daughters married noblemen in grand stately ceremonies.

However, the legacy which concerned him was not his personal triumphs but the constitutional changes he had wrought by removing a despotic and Catholic-inclined king, reforming the army, state and church. Most of these reforms were undone shortly after his death, and the returning King Charles II heaped ignominy upon defeat by having Cromwell's body dug up and posthumously executed. Cromwell's body was then decapitated, as was Ireton's, and their heads were placed on a pike above Westminster Hall, where Charles I had been tried, for several years. To this day, there are still debates over the location of Cromwell's head, and whether it is actually in someone's private possession.

A contemporary depiction of the posthumous executions of Cromwell, John Bradshaw, and Ireton

Despite the restoration, however, and despite the fact England's republican experiment barely outlasted Cromwell, the Commonwealth and Restoration were hugely important in asserting the power of Parliament, and it permanently shifted England's political balance firmly towards a constitutional monarchy limited by Parliament. The Stuart monarchy was restored on condition of compromise with Parliament and the army, and a precedent had been set for Parliament to replace the monarch, a precedent it would follow in the 1680s when James II was replaced by William and Mary in a settlement that set even more limits around the monarch. In that sense, Oliver Cromwell, who was king in all but name, helped prepare the way for monarchs who would become national leaders in name only.

On the religious front, Puritanism would never become the dominant form of religious and political thought that Cromwell wanted. His efforts to enforce its strictures did as much to turn people against the Puritans as to convert them, and Cromwell never appreciated that most of the ordinary English were not looking for moral direction but instead looking for life to be made easier and for the freedom to get drunk and celebrate Christmas. In fact, those with strict religious inclinations would have more impact in the New World than at home. The English church would soon restore much of its pomp and tradition, and English culture would once again embrace maypoles and noisy public holidays.

In the end, though the modern age embraces Cromwell's egalitarian instincts, it also embodies the need for a figurehead that brought his efforts low. It is easier for people to understand the English Civil Wars in terms of the actions of a great man than as the diverse and tumultuous mess that they really were. Cromwell provides them with that figurehead, a single person through whom to understand the struggle against Charles I, and that is perhaps his greatest legacy.

Bibliography

Braddick, Michael (2008), *God's Fury, England's Fire: A New History of the English Civil Wars*.

Duncan, Mike (2014), *Revolutions* podcast.

Isemonger, Paul Lewis (1995), *The English Civil War: A Living History* (revised edition).

Hill, Christopher (1980), *The Century of Revolution* (second edition).

Roberts, Keith (2005), *Cromwell's War Machine: The New Model Army 1645-1660*.

Schama, Simon (2001), *A History of Britain: The British Wars 1603-1776*.

Sherwood, Roy (1997), *Oliver Cromwell: King in all But Name 1653-1658*.

Made in the USA
Lexington, KY
05 November 2018